Celebrate All Colors

by Parul L. Bhandari

To request permission, contact the publisher at:
publisher@innerpeacepress.com

ISBN: 978-1-958150-75-7
Celebrate All Colors: An American-born, Indian-Heritage
Family Celebrates Holi

First edition: February 2025
Printed in U.S.A.

Published by Inner Peace Press
Eau Claire, Wisconsin
www.innerpeacepress.com

To Jaiyen, my cheerleader and creative partner,
you make celebrating fun and meaningful.

To Kishyn, my sous chef and our chief-excitement-officer;
you make celebrating exciting and worthwhile.

To Samit, my constant source of yin and yang,
you bring color to our family life every day.

To Dadi, our culture advocate, thank you for making
everything worth remembering, doing, and nurturing.

To Dada, our youngster-at-heart, thank you for being
a great advocate of all things.

To Mom and Dad, my culture champions, thank you for
building the foundations for culture and community in our lives.

To Shimul, my partner-in-culture for our next
generations and theirs to come.

To my brothers, sibs-in-law, and nieces and nephews,
thank you for the support and love always.

Hi, I am Jaiyen, and I am 6 years old.
I live in Chicago with my family.

Chicago is known as the "windy city" and
is home to the Willis Tower, one of the
tallest buildings in the world. Chicago is also
a fun place to celebrate festivals from
around the world, like St. Patrick's Day,
Dia de los Muertos, Christmas, and one
of my favorite holidays, Holi.

My brother Kishyn is 4, and together
we are starting our Holi celebrations.

Would you like to learn about Holi with us?

Holi is usually in the spring. I remember because it's near our school spring break. It is also called the Festival of Colors, because people throw colored powder on friends and family. It's pretty messy, pretty colorful, and pretty fun!

My Mama says Holi is a time when we pray for a good spring harvest for the farmers. We also pray for all the spring colors to arrive after a grey winter.

This makes me think of colorful spring flowers, and I imagine how the Holi colors are similar. I am excited for our celebrations to come.

Holi usually starts on a special day called **Punam**, which is the first night of the full moon. But in Chicago, our family celebrates Holi a few different times with friends, school, and our community!

Thinking of people throwing Holi colors reminds me of snowball fights in winter, but much brighter.

The first time we celebrated Holi this year was on the "real" Holi Day. We went to my Dadi and Dada's house after school. They are my Papa's parents and live a few minutes drive away.

When we got there, we gathered around a small puja. Dadi lit a small diya and some agarbati (uh-gur-BAH-tee) which smelled like flowers, and then Dada led us as we prayed to Ganesha, Krishna, and Radha. It was not as big of a puja as we usually do at Diwali, but it was nice. We also did a tika, which is a small red mark on our forehead which Dada says brings good energy for the gods and for us. We all closed our eyes and prayed, and offered the gods some yummy barfis.

After the puja, Dadi popped a barfi into
my mouth and said, "Happy Holi!"
I gave her and Dada a big hug.

Then we went out to the balcony, and covered
our clothes with towels. Dadi brought out a
tray of holi colors, all bright and powdery. We
dipped our fingers in and smeared the colors on
each other's faces softly. It was so fun.

I put so much blue color on Kishyn, and
he smeared purple on me. Dadi also
put green on mama's cheek.

Afterwards, we all went inside and wiped our faces off before dinner. Then we got to try a special drink, called thandai (THUHN-dye). Dadi said it was a "kid version" so we could try it. It was sweet and tingly, and a little bit spicy. I didn't love it but Mama did.

What is Holi like in India, Kishyn asked?

"Oh my" Dadi said with a smile. "Holi is like no other time in India. When I was growing up, it was the most vibrant time of the year. Every year we would do a puja the day before Holi, on a full moon night. There would be a big bonfire called dahan (DUH-hun) and the priests would burn bad energy away. Holi is also a time to pray for good over evil, just like Diwali in a way, so the puja focuses on that."

Dadi continued. "Then on Holi, we would wake up, shower, cover our bodies with oil, and wear all white. The oil would nourish our skin, but it would also make the Holi colors stain us less. The courtyard of the house would have trays of colors, and buckets of pichkaris (pich-KAA-reez), which are water shooters.

From the moment we stepped into the courtyard or out of our house, colors would be thrown all around. From the elders to the babies, everyone had a little Holi color on them. We played Holi with everyone, no matter their role in the household. It was a day to spread color and joy on everyone we came across.

We would drink Thandai, eat Gujjia (GOO-jyah), and play with our friends all day. Then in the evening we would wash all the colors off, and hope that we did not end up with a red-stained face for school the next day.

It was a lot of fun, and something we really don't do in America in the same way," said Dadi, with a faraway look in her eyes.

"Wow, that just sounds like a big mess!" Kishyn said, which made everyone laugh, including Dadi.

We finished up our dinner and headed home for a day of rest and school, just like Dadi did after her Holi celebrations.

Later that weekend, we met up with some of our
friends from school at a local park for a Holi event.
Mama had bought the whole family white
sweatshirts to wear for the day, and most people
were also wearing white. Some aunties had set up a
table with snacks, and we did a little crafting while
people arrived. Then, someone opened up a box of Holi
colors, and we all got to play Holi! People were
throwing colors all around and spreading them on
each other, just like in Dadi's story.

It was so fun, and very messy, but
Mama and Papa didn't seem to mind.

After the fun was over, we cleaned up and got in the car to drive home.

"I think Dadi would have liked that." I said.

Mama looked up and said, "You know what Jaiyen, I think you are right. She would have." She looked at Papa, and said, "maybe there is another chance for her to get to throw colors like she did in India?" Papa said, "Yes there may be." and they both smiled. "Good idea Jaiyen, we will work on a plan."

That made me happy, even though I didn't exactly know what the plan was.

The next weekend we wore our white shirts again, which were not exactly white anymore, and we picked up Dadi and Dada for a special adventure. While we were in the car, I told Dadi about the school Holi event, and she was so happy that we had played real Holi. "Did you learn about the story of Holi as well," she asked?

"Not really," I said. "Dadi, what is the story of Holi?"

Dadi explained it to me. "There are many stories of Holi, beta. But one of the main stories is a celebration of the love between Krishna and Radha, who were forms of god on earth and best friends.

Krishna was known to have darker skin than others around him. In fact that is what his name means. "Krishna" is the word for dark in Sanskrit. Even though Krishna was a god in human form, the color of his skin made him feel different when he played with friends, like his best friend Radha.

He asked his Mama what to do to feel less different, and she suggested playfully throwing colors on Radha, so their skin color would not show as much. So Krishna playfully splattered colors on Radha, which she did back to him in a sign of acceptance. This was the first Holi festival.

Now, playing colors at Holi is known as a way to show love and to be accepting of others, no matter their differences."

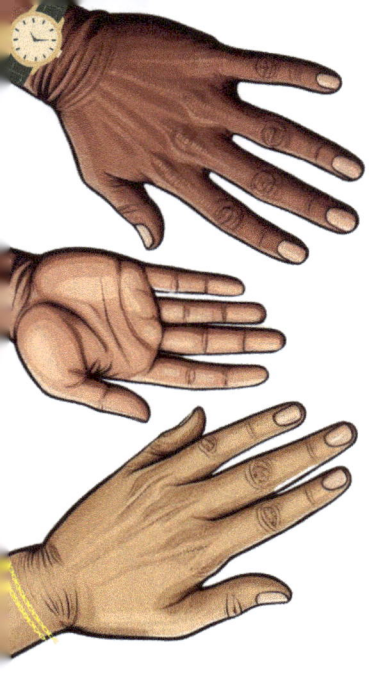

I looked down at my hand. my skin is a little bit different than other friends of mine. and even darker brown than my cousin Parisa. and Kishyn too.

"Mama. can I be like Krishna and do the same thing? Can I spread colors on Parisa and Kishyn. since my skin is darker than theirs?"

Mama smiled and said. "Well. when it comes to spreading colors. you can during Holi and only if they are ok with it. But otherwise. you can share your love in other ways. such as by being kind.

As far as your skin. look around the car. we all have different skin tones. and it's what makes us unique and special. The darkness of Krishna's skin made him feel different. which can be tough. But. Krishna lived a long time ago. and today we know a lot more about how our differences make us stronger. Differences can even make us feel proud.

For example, your skin is a mix of your mama's family and your papa's family — its golden tones glow in the sun and protect you from getting burned, and the brown tones share that you have Indian heritage.

Your skin is special because it is yours alone, but actually it protects your body the same as any other person in the world's skin does.

"So my skin makes me different, and also the same," I asked?

"Yes," said Papa, "that's right. The same goes for my skin, Kishyn's skin, and every human. That makes the world colorful. And, in a way, Holi is about celebrating all colors equally."

"Ok," I said pensively. "Everyone's skin is special, sooo... I won't throw colors all over Parisa and Kishyn, I will throw colors on everyone equally."

That made everyone in the car laugh.

Soon after, we arrived at Navy Pier, a fun place on the waterfront in Chicago, which we visit a lot on weekends. Navy pier is a really big building, with a ferris wheel, games, and lots of things to do.

We walked through a long hallway and finally ended up at the end of the building, where there was a surprise! A big Holi party was happening right in front of us! I looked at Dadi and Dada's surprised and smiling faces, taking in the colorful scene.

We all bought some colors and joined in the fun. This time, we didn't worry about towels on our clothes. We threw colors all over each other. Dadi and Dada were laughing and throwing colors too.

Dadi came over to me and put
some colors on my cheek.

I laughed and said, "Were you surprised Dadi?
Does this remind you of Holi in India when
you were a kid?"

Dadi smiled and said, "Yes beta, it is exactly like
that. Thank you for bringing me here."

Dadi and I hugged each other, then we got
back to the fun for a while.

The next morning, my head was still swirling, thinking of all the things I had learned about Holi. I have so many new favorites, from spraying pichkaris, to eating gujjia, to my most favorite, being like Krishna and spreading kindness through Holi colors.

I hope you had fun celebrating with us.

See you again next year!

ABOUT HOLI

Holi is a Hindu festival which takes place in spring and is characterized by celebrations and community. It includes a bonfire the evening before and the throwing of colored water and powder on the day of. Often called the Festival of Colors, it celebrates a bright spring and good harvest ahead. It also celebrates good over evil and accepting differences among the people around us.

ABOUT HOLI COLORS

Blue represents Krishna's divine gifts and the color of his skin, which is said to be dark, bluish-black. Blue color used to come from indigo powder.

Red/Pink symbolizes love and fertility and is often seen as a symbol of marriage, which is highly valued in India. Red color used to come from fruits like pomogranate or flowers like roses.

Yellow is the color of turmeric, which is an ancient and auspicious spice in Hinduism. Yellow color used to come from marigolds or from the turmeric root.

Green is the color of spring and promotes growth and a fresh perspective. Green color used to come from henna, or dried leaves.

RELEVANT MYTHOLOGICAL STORIES

Holi is rooted in several Hindu mythological stories, including the tale of Prahlad and Holika. In this story, an evil king seeks to harm his virtuous son, Prahlad, who was a faithful worshiper of Vishnu the God of Creation. His aunt, Holika, was granted immunity from fire in from a previous deed. One day, the king asked her to sit with Prahlad on a pyre, believing she would remain unharmed, while the child would perish.

However, Prahlad's unwavering devotion to Vishnu, the God of Creation, protected him, while Holika perished instead. This event symbolizes the triumph of good over evil. Holi Dahan, or the ceremonial bonfire, serves as a reminder to do the right thing.

Another popular Holi legend is the story of Kamadeva, the God of Love. After losing his wife, Shiva, the God of Destruction, withdrew into deep meditation, disrupting the world's balance. Though his wife was reborn as Parvati, Shiva remained unmoved. To restore harmony, Kamadeva bravely shot an arrow of love at Shiva, not to harm him, but to awaken his heart. Though he knew this act would anger Shiva and bring punishment upon himself, Kamadeva sacrificed for the greater good. In some parts of India, the Holi bonfire symbolizes Kamadeva's sacrifice in the name of love and balance.

RELEVANT MYTHOLOGICAL STORIES

Another tale tells of Krishna and Radha, best friends and soulmates. Despite being a divine incarnation, Krishna feels self-conscious about his darker skin compared to Radha's. Sensing his anxiety, Krishna's mother suggests playing with Holi colors, allowing them to blur the differences and celebrate their bond. This story highlights Holi as a festival of unity, reminding us to embrace diversity and look beyond appearances.

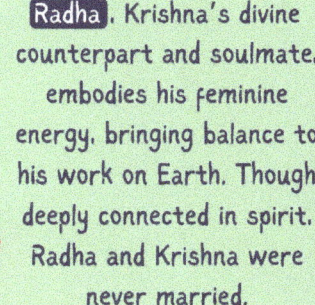

Radha, Krishna's divine counterpart and soulmate, embodies his feminine energy, bringing balance to his work on Earth. Though deeply connected in spirit, Radha and Krishna were never married.

Krishna, the eighth avatar of Vishnu, the God of Creation, was put on Earth to guide humanity through its challenges and inspire self-discovery. He is portrayed as both a playful trickster and a powerful warrior, as well as a wise and compassionate counselor.

Fun fact: Krishna is often depicted playing a flute, symbolizing harmony and the enchanting power of his music. He also wears a peacock feather in his crown or turban, representing wisdom, even though he is frequently portrayed as a child.

ABOUT PUJAS

Ganesha, the remover of obstacles, is the first deity invoked in Hindu rituals, ensuring a smooth path for any endeavor by clearing hurdles and bringing blessings.

Punam is the word for full moon, also called purnima or poonam. It is often associated with auspicious days in the lunar calendar.

Agarbati is the Hindi word for incense. It is traditionally used in pujas and ceremonies to purify the space, create a sacred atmosphere, and honor God through its fragrant offering.

A **Diya** is a small, traditional oil lamp usually made of clay. It is lit during pujas, Diwali, and other festivals, symbolizing light, purity, and the triumph of good over evil.

Tika is a ceremonial mark on the forehead, usually made our of dried red flower powder called **Kumkum**. It is applied to create energy and symbolizes readiness for a prayer or task ahead.

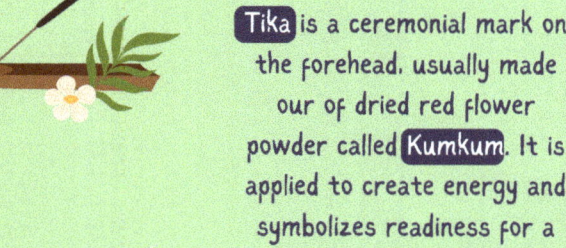

Puja is a religious ceremony when Hindus pray to God by gathering around an image of God, performing rituals to purify and cleanse, and then praying and singing. Pujas can be performed in the temple or at home. The rituals often involve offering food to God, and then partaking in the **prasad** or blessed food to bless yourself. There are similar rituals in Christianity and other religions. Puja plates, or **thalis**, are typically set up with all of the offerings.

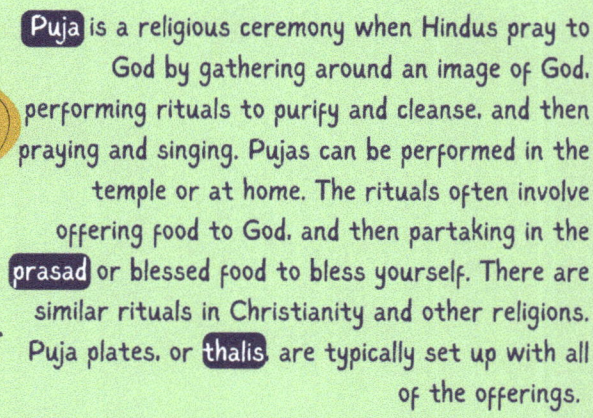

FUN & FOOD

Pichkaris are water pistols commonly used during Holi to spray colored water on others.

Beta is a word for a child, or younger person, when spoken by an elder.

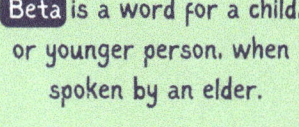

Barfis are small sweets made of flour, cheese, or nuts. They are usually cooked and molded into small square or diamond shapes.

Gujjia are small sweet pastries, wrapped and fried until golden brown. They are usually filled with sweetened nut mixtures. They are a Holi specialty.

Thandai is a drink made of milk and almonds, with spices like fennel and black pepper. It is intended to cool the body from the inside, hence the word "thand" which means cold, in its name.

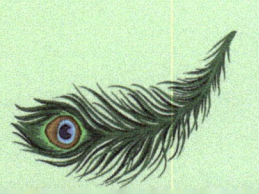

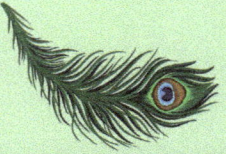

Jaiyen's Dadi's Coconut Barfi Recipe

Ingredients

- 1 1/2 cup ricotta cheese
- 1/3 cup oat (or almond) flour
- 3/4 cup sugar
- 1 tsp cardamom
- 1 pinch of salt
- 1/2 cup unsweetened coconut flakes
- almonds for garnish (optional)

Directions

Mix ricotta, flour, sugar, cardamom, and salt together in a pan. Cook on medium heat until well combined and the water somewhat evaporates and the dough binds. Turn off heat and add coconut flakes. Spread on parchment paper about 1/2 inch thick and let cool (spread almond garnish on top if you like). Cut into 1.5 X 1.5 inch squares and serve.

DIY Pichkari (Water Blaster) Decoration

Materials Needed

- Empty paper towel roll
- Colored paper or paints
- Glue and tape
- Glitter, sequins, or stickers for decoration
- Ribbon or yarn
- 1 paper straw

Instructions

- Start with a plain paper towel roll.
- Prepare the base
  - Paint the paper towel roll in bright Holi colors or wrap it in colored paper.
  - Cover one end with a cone of paper (the nozzle).
  - Cut a small round paper slightly larger than the diameter of the pichkari and puncture a small hole in it (keep to the side).
- Decorate
  - Use glitter, stickers, or sequins to add fun patterns and festive designs.
- Create a Pusher
  - Cut a straw 1/3 of the way down, and secure it together in a "T" shape with the long piece attaching to the center of the short piece.
  - Attach the pusher to your round paper by taping it to the inside of the paper, through the hole.
  - Attach the cover to the end of the pichkari with glue or tape (opposite the nozzle).
- Attach ribbon to the nozzle to look like streaming colored water.

HAPPY HOLI

About the Author

Parul L. Bhandari is a woman, born in the U.S. to first generation immigrants from India. Growing up, culture and rituals, especially around Diwali and Holi, were anticipated and celebrated with the community.

When Parul started visiting her children's classrooms as an adult, it was to share this culture beyond her family walls. Her first book, "Shine a Light on Diwali" was published in 2024, and shares stories of their American-heritage experience during Diwali season. Similarly, this book on Holi was inspired by various Holi celebrations in and around her modern life.

Parul is also a Customer Experience consultant, South Asian professional community leader, and a columnist for Inc.com. Her love of writing started at a young age, and has touched many forms such as poetry, fiction, and business writing.

Parul lives in Chicago with her husband and is "Mama" to her own Jaiyen and Kishyn.

Follow along with her journey at
www.parullbhandari.com

www.ingramcontent.com/pod-product-compliance
Lightning Source LLC
Chambersburg PA
CBHW051337120626
46547CB00016B/2591